DANIEL

Our Faithful God

Andrew Reid and
Karen Morris

FAITHWALK
BIBLE STUDIES

CROSSWAY BOOKS • WHEATON, ILLINOIS
A DIVISION OF GOOD NEWS PUBLISHERS

Contents

How to Make the Most of These Studies

1. What Is an Interactive Bible Study?

These "interactive" Bible studies are a bit like a guided tour of a famous city. The studies will take you through Daniel, pointing out things along the way, filling in background details, and suggesting avenues for further exploration. But there is also time for you to do some sightseeing of your own—to wander off, have a good look for yourself, and form your own conclusions.

In other words, we have designed these studies to fall halfway between a sermon and a set of unadorned Bible study questions. We want to provide stimulation and input and point you in the right direction, while leaving you to do a lot of the exploration and discovery yourself.

We hope that these studies will stimulate lots of interaction—interaction with the Bible, with the things we've written, with your own current thoughts and attitudes, with other people as you study with them, and with God as you talk to Him about it all.

2. The Format

Each study contains sections of text to introduce, summarize, suggest, and provoke. Interspersed throughout the text are three types of "interaction," each with its own symbol:

STARTING OUT
Questions to break the ice and get you thinking.

FINDING TRUTH
Questions to help you investigate key parts of the Bible.

GOING FURTHER
Questions to help you think through the implications of your discoveries.

When you come to one of these symbols, you'll know that it's time to do some work on your own.

3. Suggestions for Individual Study

▲ Before you begin, pray that God will open your eyes to what He is saying in Daniel, and give you the spiritual strength to do something about it. You may be spurred to pray again at the end of the study.

▲ Work through the study, following the directions as you go. Write in the spaces provided.

▲ Resist the temptation to skip over the *Going Further* sections. It is important to think about the sections of text (rather than just accepting them as true) and to ponder the implications for your life. Writing these things down is a very valuable way to get your thoughts working.

▲ Take what opportunities you can to talk with others about what you have learned.

4. Suggestions for Group Study

▲ Many of the above suggestions apply to group study as well. The studies are suitable for structured Bible study or cell groups, as well as for more informal pairs or threesomes. Get together with one or more friends and work on the studies at your own pace. You don't need the formal structure of a "group" to gain maximum benefit.

▲ It is vital that group members work through the study themselves *before* the group meets. The group discussion can take place comfortably in an hour (depending on how sidetracked you get!), but only if all the members have done the work and are familiar with the material.

▲ Spend most of the group time discussing the "interactive" sections—*Starting Out, Finding Truth* and *Going Further.* Reading all the text together would take too long and should be unnecessary if the group members have done their preparation. You may wish to underline and read aloud particular paragraphs or sections of text that you think are important.

▲ The role of the group leader is to direct the course of the discussion and try to draw the threads together at the end. This will mean a little extra preparation—underlining important sections of text to emphasize, deciding which questions are worth concentrating on, and being sure of the main thrust of the study. Leaders will also probably want to decide approximately how long they'd like to spend on each part.

▲ We haven't included an "answer guide" to the questions in the studies. This is a deliberate move. We want to give you a guided tour of Daniel, not a lecture. There is more than enough in the text we have written and the questions we have asked to point you in what we think is the right direction. The rest is up to you.

Before You Begin

We recommend that before you start on study 1, you take the time to read right through Daniel in one sitting. This will give you a feel for the direction and purpose of the whole book and help you greatly in looking at each passage in its context.

Getting Started

The first study is deliberately short to introduce you to the context of the book of Daniel. If you are studying this book in a group setting, you may want to use the extra time as a "get acquainted" session or prayer time, or to discuss how you will function as a group.

1

Getting Some Perspective

DANIEL 1:1-2

 STARTING OUT

If you are studying in a group, start with a large piece of paper or poster board and draw a straight line with the word *Creation* at one end and *Jesus* at the other end:

Creation   Jesus

On the last page of this first study, you will find a list of people, passages, and events from the Old Testament. Photocopy the page and then cut out the pieces. Hand them around the group so that each person has a mixture of pieces.

Go around the group and ask each participant who has a PEOPLE piece to put it at the appropriate place on the "Creation to Jesus" line, and to share with the group anything they know about the person named. This is a "whole group experience," so everyone can help. The aim is simply to get the names in some sort of order.

Once the PEOPLE pieces are on the paper, link up the *PASSAGES* and *EVENTS* pieces with them, explaining how they connect with each other. Feel free to check the references in your Bible.

If you are studying on your own, you may simply want to draw lines connecting the people with the correct Bible passages, and then connect those passages with the events they describe.

When God called Abraham in Genesis 12, He promised him three great things: 1) a land; 2) that he would be a great nation; and 3) that He would bless him and cause him to be a blessing to all the world. By the beginning of the book of Exodus, Abraham's children have indeed become great in number, however they are in captivity in Egypt and far from the land of God's promise.

The books of Exodus through Joshua tell how God rescues His people from Egypt, enters into covenant with them, and brings them into the land He had promised to Abraham. At first things go well and God rules His people directly, through Spirit-filled leaders called "judges"—as recorded in the book of Judges. However, the Israelites become unhappy with these sorts of leaders and ask God for a more steady sort of leadership such as a king would offer (1 Sam. 8). Although God knows that such a request really amounts to a rejection of His kingship over Israel, He allows them to have a king and even makes an eternal covenant with King David, promising him that his children will always rule over God's people (2 Sam. 7).

Soon after David, the institution of kingship fails and Israel is split in two: ten tribes in the north ruled by a series of various kings, and two tribes in the south ruled by the descendants of David. The ten tribes in the north (called Israel) turn against God, and He eventually punishes them, using the kingdom of Assyria. The two tribes in the south (called Judah) don't act any better. Eventually God judges them as well, this time by means of Nebuchadnezzar, king of Babylon. Nebuchadnezzar overthrows Judah and carts the nation off into exile. It is these events that set the context for the book of Daniel.

 **FINDING TRUTH**

Read 2 Kings 25:1-21 and Daniel 1:1-2.

1. Describe in your own words the events recorded in these passages.

2. Psalm 137 was written about the Israelites' experience in the Exile. What does it tell you about the way the Israelites were feeling in exile? (If you want to do some more study on this, you could also read the short book of Lamentations.)

3. Spend some time praying about the following studies on Daniel. Include these sorts of things in your prayers:

   ▲ Pray for insight and understanding as to what the book of Daniel means.

   ▲ Pray for wisdom to know how to apply it to your own situation.

   ▲ If you are studying in a group, pray for good working relationships with each other so that you can gain the most benefit from the studies and be supportive of each other.

   ▲ Pray for opportunities to use what you learn in your conversations with other people.

Match These People, Bible Passages, and Events:

People	Passages	Events
DAVID	1 Kings 8	Promise of return from exile
ISAIAH	Exodus 6:6-8	God's covenant promise
JOSHUA	Jeremiah 27:22; 31:31-33	Entry into the Promised Land
SOLOMON	Daniel 1	Temple established
DANIEL	2 Samuel 7:1-17	Creation
JEREMIAH	Deuteronomy 34:4-9	Promise of Exodus from Egypt
ADAM	Isaiah 39:1-8	Promise of the Exile
ABRAM	Genesis 12:1-3	Kingship
MOSES	Genesis 2:15-17	Living in exile

2

So . . . Do You Fit In?

DANIEL 1

Emaciated, hollow-eyed, and despairing. Last night I saw again the photographs and black and white films recording the Holocaust. At times I'm tempted to think that this was a dark part of human history that could never be repeated. But the strikingly similar photos of piles of skulls dug up after the exploits of Pol Pot, mass graves in Bosnia and Herzegovina, and cut-up bodies in Rwanda show that we humans still have the ability to wage war with gruesome violence and monstrous cruelty.

These pictures are testimony to one of the difficulties any victorious side in war has with the vanquished: How should it handle the land and the people it has conquered? What should it do with the subjugated people? How can it retain its power over them?

 STARTING OUT

1.   List as many wars (ancient or modern) as you can in one minute.

2. When one nation defeats another, what are some of the methods used in dealing with the subjects and property of the conquered nation?

3. Read Daniel 1.

The opening verses of Daniel set the context for the book. They tell us that the book is set on a global stage, involving whole nations. At the same time it is also set on a personal stage, involving particular representatives of those nations.

The Global Stage: Daniel 1:1-7

There are three telltale phrases in the first couple of verses of Daniel 1. These phrases pose very significant questions that the rest of the chapter and even the rest of the book set out to answer. The first phrase tells us that "the Lord delivered Jehoiakim king of Judah" into the hands of Nebuchadnezzar king of Babylon. In other words, it is God who has been at work to bring about Judah's disastrous state of affairs. He is active, but His activity has taken a strange turn in that it appears that He has turned His face away from His people.

The second phrase tells us that Nebuchadnezzar not only defeated the nation but also took some of the articles from the temple of God in Jerusalem, and these he "carried off to the temple of his god in Babylonia." The point is that, not only has God apparently turned away from His people, but He seems to have been devastatingly defeated. Surely no God who is really powerful would allow both His people and the symbols of His glory to be so demeaningly captured by other gods and their representatives.

The third telltale phrase is less evident without some detailed background knowledge. Verse 2 tells us that the articles from God's temple are deposited in the temple of Nebuchadnezzar's god "in Babylonia"; some versions, and the NIV marginal reading, refer to "Shinar" rather than Babylonia. The reference to Babylonia or Shinar goes back to the Tower of Babel in Genesis 11. The Tower of Babel is a biblical symbol of human arrogance, of human kingdoms setting themselves against God's kingdom. By using this phrase, the author reminds us that Nebuchadnezzar is, in effect, setting himself against God.

Hence, after only two verses, we as readers have a whole lot of questions running through our minds: Is God defeated? How is He going to deal with this situation? Will He take on the gods of Babylon? Will He demonstrate His power by rescuing His people? Will He "do a Babel" again? These verses and these questions set the agenda for the book. It is a book about Babylon versus Israel and the gods of the nations versus the God of Israel.

 GOING FURTHER

1. Of the various policies of war and conquest that you talked about above, which one does Nebuchadnezzar appear to be following?

    ▲ What is Nebuchadnezzar trying to do?

    ▲ What particular actions taken in this passage indicate that this is his policy?

    (A note of explanation: The names of the four young men are Hebrew names that also contain Hebrew names of God. "Daniel," for instance, means "God is my judge." The names Nebuchadnezzar gives the men incorporate the names of Babylonian gods.)

2. Imagine you were a young Jew in the Exile. How do you think you would react to the situation and to Nebuchadnezzar's actions?

To understand the stories of Daniel and his friends in Babylon it is necessary to understand some of the factors affecting these four men. Every Jew in Babylon knew why he or she was there. Their ancestors had been given commandments by God, the first two of which were:

> *"You shall have no other gods before me"*.
>
> —Exodus 20:3, RSV

and

> *"You shall not make for yourself a graven image, or any likeness of anything that is in heaven above, or that is in the earth beneath, or that is in the water under the earth; you shall not bow down to them or serve them; for I the LORD your God am a jealous God, visiting the iniquity of the fathers upon the children to the third and fourth generation of those who hate me, but showing steadfast love to thousands of those who love me and keep my commandments."*
>
> —Exodus 20:4-6, RSV

These two commandments lay at the root of the Israelites' faith, and at the root of their sin and their exile in Babylon. Because of their failure to keep these two commandments, they are suffering judgment in exile. As a result of their sin in this area, they are experiencing God's anger and punishment, just as He had promised they would if they continued to sin (see Lev. 26:38-39; Deut. 28:45-50; 1 Kings 9:6-9).

This explains the resolve of Daniel and his friends. They are determined that they will not repeat the failure of their ancestors. They will be loyal and obedient to God and to His commandments at any cost. They will not jettison their identity as Israelites and as worshipers of the true and living God.

The Personal Stage: Daniel 1:8-17

 FINDING TRUTH

1. Daniel accepts a Babylonian education and a name change, but then resolves "not to defile himself with the royal food and wine." What could be wrong with the food and wine?

    (After thinking about this, see if the following passages help: Psalm 41:9; John 13:18.)

2. What statement is Daniel making by his refusal to eat the Babylonian food? For whose benefit is he doing it?

3. Why do you think Daniel is doing this and what made it so important to him?

4. How does God respond to Daniel's act?

The God Who Is Present and Active

There are three references to God's actions in the chapter. We have already seen the first one in verse 2, where we are told that it is by God's will and action that Israel finds itself in Babylon. The second occurs in verse 9, where God causes the official to show favor and sympathy to Daniel. The third reference comes in verse 17, where God acts to give "these four young men . . . knowledge and understanding of all kinds of literature and learning."

Remember the first few verses? They were markedly despondent. God looked defeated. He had handed His people over to a pagan king, and the vessels from His temple were deposited in the temple of Nebuchadnezzar's gods. The Babylonians and their gods undoubtedly had the upper hand.

However, by the end of the chapter things have changed completely. God has rescued Daniel, and the Babylonians and their gods have been shown to be no match for God and His people. As though to demonstrate this beyond any doubt, the writer concludes the chapter by telling us that Daniel remained in the king's service right up to the time when Babylon fell to Cyrus, king of Persia.

God's means for defeating the Babylonians is not what we expect. We expect Him to shatter Babylon with superior force of arms or devastating judgment as He did on the plain of Shinar with the Tower of Babel in Genesis 11. Instead, the defeat comes through Daniel and his friends' determination to resist assimilation, to be faithful to their God, and to take risks where necessary to preserve their identity as God's people.

 **GOING FURTHER**

1. What is so important about being God's people?

2. In what areas are our faith and identity as God's people put in jeopardy?

3. What actions can we take to ensure that this identity is not taken away from us or put at risk?

4. Where do you personally compromise your faith? What changes do you need to put into place that will help you remain faithful?

5. Pray that God will be active as you make those changes, and that He will help you to remain faithful to Him.

Captains and Teams

DANIEL 2

Nebuchadnezzar must have been an awesome man to meet. He was born of a royal line and prepared for kingship from his birth. Even in his youth it was evident that he had inherited and even surpassed the considerable military skill and cunning of his father, Nabopolassar. When he became king, he had continued and exceeded his father's program of military campaigns. Vast tributes were collected, and huge numbers of captives were brought to Babylonia.

He was a reasonably good king at home. He dispensed justice, opposed hostile kings attempting to rob his regions of riches, reunited scattered fugitive people, and made the whole land happy.

On top of this he engaged in massive building projects. He reconstructed the main river wall and quay, and began to plan a series of hydraulic works that would counter the eastward drift of the Euphrates. The palace he would build later in his reign would be magnificent. The upper walls would be decorated around with a band of blue enameled bricks; the doors would be made of the best cedar, magan, sissoo, or ebony wood and would be encased in bronze or inlaid with silver, gold, and ivory. The doorway ceilings would be coated with lapis lazuli, and the thresholds, lintels, and moldings would be cast in bronze. Outside the palace there would be royal terraced gardens housing a museum and looking out over the parkland.

Nebuchadnezzar was a very impressive man. It appeared that nothing could threaten or shake him. But then came this dream.

 **STARTING OUT**

Read Daniel 2.

The World of Dreams

The book of Daniel contains many references to dreams. There are dreams by Daniel and dreams by people such as Nebuchadnezzar. In our modern world dreams are considered to be the gateway to an inner world. They inform us in visual language about repressed experiences and other processes of the unconscious. For the people of the ancient world, however, the realm of dreams was viewed very differently. For them dreams provided a window into the world of the gods. To dream was to have a communication from the gods.

Archaeological digs in Babylon and Egypt have unearthed a large number of "dream manuals." These manuals contained long lists of dreams and their meanings. Once in possession of the content of the dream, the interpretation came easily.

Nebuchadnezzar knew this. For this reason perhaps he was glad that he could not recall his dream. Perhaps he thought that if there were someone who knew the content of the dream itself, then that person could be trusted to give a faithful interpretation. On the other hand, perhaps Nebuchadnezzar did remember the dream but chose to hide it from his band of astrologers and wise men, in hopes of finding someone who could give a true interpretation.

 FINDING TRUTH

Divide the people in your study group into two opposing groups. One group will represent Nebuchadnezzar and the astrologers. The other group will represent Daniel and his friends. On the basis of Daniel chapter 2, answer the following questions.

(If you are studying Daniel on your own you can do this exercise by completing both sections separately.)

Nebuchadnezzar and the Astrologers

▲ List the attributes of the god/s this group believes in.

▲ How do the gods act in the world?

▲ How does this group think about other humans (including how they relate to each other and to God)?

▲ Create a motto or slogan for Nebuchadnezzar and the astrologers that summarizes their overall approach to life and reality.

Daniel and His Friends

▲ List the attributes of the God this group believes in.

▲ How does God act in the world?

▲ How does this group think about other humans (including how they relate to each other and to God)?

▲ Create a motto or slogan for Daniel and his friends that summarizes their overall approach to life and reality.

Bring the two groups back together. Share what you found and show where in the passage you got your information. Perhaps, in order to really get into the idea of opposing views of reality, each team could present its report in terms of "We believe . . ." rather than "The astrologers believed . . ." or "Daniel and his friends believed . . ."

Caught in Cosmic Conflict

In Daniel 2, we see two views of the world in conflict. On the one hand, there are Daniel and his friends. They know they have been brought to Babylon according to God's will (Dan. 1:2). Moreover, they see themselves as God's representatives. They represent a view of the world in which there is only one God and He is the rightful ruler of all the world. But they don't represent this view in a vacuum. They are surrounded, in Babylon, by the best in ancient wisdom and learning and attitudes toward things divine. Daniel and his friends are caught up in a conflict or contest between two kingdoms or worldviews.

However, when we read the chapter closely we see that both Daniel and his friends, and Nebuchadnezzar and his astrologers, are representatives of their respective gods. The real contest is not between them but between the God of Israel and the gods of the nations.

 GOING FURTHER

If we are Christians, then we too are God's representatives—and we too are surrounded by alternative views of God and the world.

1. In what areas is the conflict between these alternative views most obvious and clear? List some of the most common statements that represent these worldviews.

2. Can you think of some more subtle ways in which the Christian worldview is attacked? Write down some statements that demonstrate these subtle attacks. Discuss ways of responding to each of these.

3. How should we react to this conflict? In what practical ways can we be like Daniel and his friends and take on the false gods of this world and show them up as counterfeit?

Of course the main way we "take on the false gods of this world and show them up as counterfeit" is when we preach the Gospel. When we share with other people the great news about who God is and what He has done in Jesus Christ, and they respond and accept Him, God is saying clearly that He is still alive and active. He is still able to turn people away from idols to serve a true and living God (1 Thess. 1:9).

This is also the case when we choose to live godly lives. Whenever we choose God's way over the world's way, we demonstrate God's victory over sin in the death of Christ.

Thinking About Statues and Images

 FINDING TRUTH

Read Genesis 1:28, Jeremiah 27:4-7, and Daniel 2:37-38.

1. What are the similarities and differences among these passages? How does God view Nebuchadnezzar in Daniel 2?

2. What should be our attitude toward governments and other authorities? (See Matt. 17:24-27; 22:15-22; Rom. 13:1-7.)

3. In what specific situations do you think it might be appropriate to defy an earthly authority? (See Acts 4:18-20; 5:27-32.)

In the ancient world a king would often set up statues or images of himself around his kingdom. These images represented the king and declared his rule. When God makes humans He makes them in His image; that is, He gives them His rule and authority (Gen. 1:27ff; Ps. 8).

Daniel 2:37-38 clearly alludes to Genesis 1:28 (as does Jeremiah 27:4-7). The implication is that Nebuchadnezzar had been given dominion over God's world just as Adam had, to rule it as God's representative.

The passage also shows clearly that, in the long run, Nebuchadnezzar's kingdom looks like a huge idol. It is idolatrous—built by human hands and resting on feet of clay. Daniel 2 tells us that against such kingdoms God will finally set His own kingdom, carved out of a mountain (i.e., carved out of Mt. Zion or Jerusalem—a Jewish kingdom), made without hands, and eternal in its rule.

Such a kingdom became visible in history with the ministry of John the Baptist (Matt. 3:2, 11-12). John the Baptist spoke in the same vein as Daniel, as he told people of a coming kingdom of God that would put an end to all human kingdoms. In Jesus—a son of David, a Jew—God would set up a kingdom made without hands that would never be destroyed. Wherever the Gospel is preached, God is hurling the rock at the kingdoms of human beings—and the day will come when He will do it one final, cataclysmic time, and on that day only *His* kingdom will remain.

 GOING FURTHER

1. If the only things and people left intact on the last day will be those that belong to God's kingdom as found in Jesus Christ, how will you fare?

2. What needs to happen to ensure that you and your work survive on the last day?

3. Where do you defy authority in government, and what needs to change in your thoughts and actions in this area?

4

Into the Fiery Furnace

DANIEL 3 and 6

Children's Stories?

If you were to walk into any Christian bookstore and browse the shelves of the children's section, you would undoubtedly find a story book about Daniel and his friends. Were you to delve into this book, past its bright colors and simple pictures, you would probably find the story of Daniel in the lion's den, or of Shadrach, Meshach, and Abednego and the fiery furnace. It has always intrigued me that we modern Christians, who turn off our televisions to protect our children from violence, read these stories to our children before just about any others. Underneath it all, I suspect that this is because we think these stories are too incredible for adults or are of no use to us.

Nothing could be further from the truth. The stories of Daniel and his friends raise some of the most complex issues of Christian faith. They talk about suffering and evil, and about a good and great God who thrusts His saints into overwhelming and awful situations. They talk about maintaining faith in the face of severe testing. They talk about the presence and absence of God in a world that is seemingly dominated by forces more powerful and visible than God Himself.

Daniel 3

 FINDING TRUTH

Read Daniel 3.

1. Why do you think Shadrach, Meshach, and Abednego act in the way they do?

2. What does Nebuchadnezzar doubt (v. 15), and what answer do Shadrach, Meshach, and Abednego give in response (vv. 16-18)?

The following alternative translation of these verses, taken from John Goldingay's *Word Bible Commentary* on Daniel, may help with this question:

> *"We do not need to make any response regarding this. If our God, whom we honor, exists, he is able to rescue us from . . . your power, your majesty. Even if he should not, your majesty may be assured that we are not going to honor your gods or bow down to the gold statue which you have set up."*

3. What do the young men expect from God in this situation?

Daniel 3 and 6 present to us people who occupy positions of great importance in Babylon. They have wealth. They have position. They have status. At the same time they are people of great godliness. Can these two truths about them coexist? Is it possible to serve the King of heaven while serving an earthly king? Is there a cost involved in serving two masters? And if there is a cost involved, then who gets shortchanged? To survive, do you have to compromise?

These are the questions that lie below the surface of excitement and drama in chapters 3 and 6 of Daniel. They are questions of crucial importance for God's people in any age, including our own, as we live in a world set against God.

The Cost and Glory of Discipleship

Christians throughout the ages have known two things to be true: on the one hand, that God is the living God who alone makes sense of the world; and on the other hand, that the world is sinful, set against God, His purposes, and His people. The end result is, the Christian knows that living for God means inevitable trouble and persecution (see 2 Tim. 3:12).

This is where the supernatural being in the furnace comes in. The important thing is not who that being is, but what God is saying through the being's presence. He is saying that, whatever happens to the godly as they stand for Him in a hostile world, He will be there with them. If we stand with Him, He will stand with us.

Daniel 6

 FINDING TRUTH

Read Daniel 6.

1. Now go back and read verses 1-18. Stop there! We know what happens at this point, but the people involved didn't know. Try and get the sense of being there with them. Perhaps the following questions will help.

   ▲ Imagine you are the king. What might you be thinking and feeling at this point?

▲ Imagine you are the officials. What might you be thinking and feeling at this point?

▲ Imagine you are Daniel. What might you be thinking and feeling at this point?

2. At the end of the story, Daniel and his God are vindicated, and God is praised. What is He praised for?

Don't Miss the Patterns!

There are some striking parallels between the story of Shadrach, Meshach, and Abednego in chapter 3 and that of Daniel in chapter 6. We could summarize these parallels under the following headings:

Belief in God costs something (see James 4:4).

Choosing to believe in God means aligning ourselves with Him and depending on Him. It means becoming a friend of God.

But there is a flip side. The world is set against God, its Creator. Therefore becoming a friend of God means becoming an enemy of the world (and those who are in it), and since God is invisible and we are visible, the people of this world will often want to take out on us their grievances against God.

We can see this in both of these stories. The friendship that these young men have with God makes them vulnerable, and such vulnerability costs them.

God assures us of His presence at all times (see 2 Tim. 2:13).

One of the essential aspects of God's character is His faithfulness. God is true or faithful; He holds us in His hand. Once He commits Himself to someone He doesn't let them go, nor does He allow anything to tear them out of His hand. Moreover, He promises that He will never leave us or forsake us no matter what happens to us. In Jesus He will be with us forever (see Ps. 46; Matt. 1:23; 28:20).

Again, although these young men didn't know Jesus, they knew that God would remain faithful to them. This is what their experiences are all about.

God will vindicate Himself and us.

Because God is faithful and true, He will always be victorious. He will always be finally vindicated. And since we have aligned ourselves with Him, we will eventually be vindicated with Him as we remain faithful to Him.

The young men are demonstrations of this. They know that God is true, and they stick with Him despite huge temptations not to do so. Eventually, although they must go through the fire, they are saved. God vindicates them, and their oppressors recognize their integrity and the power of their God.

God will rescue.

Again, because God is faithful and true He can never leave His saints. He can never be separated from them. Therefore He will eventually rescue them, as He does in both of these passages.

The patterns we see in these chapters in Daniel appear many other places in the Bible (e.g., Joseph, the Psalms of David, Esther, Jeremiah, etc.). We see them dramatically at work in the life, death, and resurrection of Jesus. The faithfulness of God's people to their God will always be taken advantage of, and will inevitably lead them into suffering and pain—and eventually to vindication.

 GOING FURTHER

Read 2 Timothy 2:11-13.

1. What principles from this passage could apply to the situations of the young men in Babylon?

Does God always rescue His people? If so, when? How? What from? If not, why not?

Read Romans 8:37-39.

2. How does this passage revise your answers to the above questions?

3. What situations have you found yourself in where you think God should rescue you? From what situations have you commonly heard Christians say God should rescue them?

What does God promise?

How do you feel about the fact that He may not always do what you want?

4. Spend some time praying, telling God what you think and feel about these things.

5

Who's the King Around Here?

DANIEL 4 and 5

The first recorded words in the public ministry of Jesus are those in Mark 1:15. Jesus says, "The time has come . . . the kingdom of God is near. Repent and believe the good news." From that moment on, nearly everything He says is colored by language of the kingdom of God. This language of kings and kingdoms is the language of the book of Daniel more so than of any other Old Testament book. We've seen this ever since we opened the first page. The book is all about rule and authority, kings and kingdoms, kingdoms of humans and the kingdom or kingship of God.

Chapters 4 and 5 continue this exploration from a slightly different perspective by taking us into the lives, minds, and attitudes of two Babylonian kings. The main players in these chapters are not God's people but foreign kings.

 STARTING OUT

1. List the various people who are "in authority" over you in the various aspects of your life.

2. How do you expect these people to act toward you in the exercise of their authority?

Daniel 4

Only a few parts of the Bible are in the first person; Daniel 4 is the only case anywhere in the Old Testament where the first person is used in a reasonably long bit of writing, and here it comes from the lips of someone who is not an Israelite. Moreover, the form is that of a royal document of great authority.

The end result is that, as we read Daniel 4, we get the feeling that what we are about to be told is very important, not only for its author but also for us (note that it is addressed to us in person—"To the peoples, nations and men of every language, who live in all the world . . ."). Here is a pagan king addressing us and telling us what he has learned about the true and living God.

 FINDING TRUTH

Read Daniel 4.

1. List all the statements Nebuchadnezzar makes about himself. These could be read out loud to emphasize their impact.

2. List all the statements made about God.

3. What picture do we get of the king from these statements?

4. What picture do we get of God?

5. What was Nebuchadnezzar's problem?

6. Why did God act in the way He did?

7. Which verse do you think gives the point of the whole chapter?

Statues and Images Again

Back in study 3 we learned about statues and images. We noticed the remarkable similarity between the language used of Adam in Genesis 1:28 and the language used of Nebuchadnezzar in Daniel 2:37-38. Adam is in the image of God in that he is to rule over the world under God's rule and as God's representative. To be truly human is therefore to rule the world acknowledging:

1. that all rule is given by God (Dan. 4:34-35); and
2. that human authority needs to be exercised as God would exercise it—with kindness and without oppression (Dan. 4:27).

This explains the incident where Nebuchadnezzar becomes a beast of the field. He had stood on the roof of his palace (a place usually associated with arrogance, self congratulation, and sin—see 2 Sam. 11) and had said, "Is not this the great Babylon I have built as the royal residence, by my mighty power and for the glory of my majesty" (4:30, emphasis added). He was no longer living as a human should before God. From God's perspective, Nebuchadnezzar was no longer seeing himself properly as a human being. It was as though he had become insane and inhuman.

This also explains Nebuchadnezzar's return from being a beast. The transformation back to sanity and humanity came when "I, Nebuchadnezzar, raised my eyes toward heaven" and acknowledged that "*His* dominion is an eternal dominion. . . . *His* kingdom endures. . . . *He* does as He pleases. . . . No one can hold back *His* hand, or say to Him: 'What have you done?'" (4:34-35, emphasis added).

 GOING FURTHER

1. Remember back to our first study: The people of Israel were in exile; they were slaves to a foreign king. What impact would this story have had on them?

2. What was the author's purpose for including this story?

3. Since this story is so specifically addressed to us, what is its message for us?

4. What difference does it make to us?

Daniel 5

 FINDING TRUTH

Read Daniel 5.

1. Record the contrasts in the chapter using the following grid.

God	The gods

2. Record the contrasts between this chapter and chapter 4.

Astrologers	Daniel
Nebuchadnezzar	**Belshazzar**

3. *(Optional)* Read through Psalm 145 and list the characteristics of God's kingship.

4. *(Optional)* Isaiah 52:13-53 appears to be talking about a king-like figure. How does this king-like person exercise his rule?

5. How does Jesus exercise His rule (Mark 10:35-45) and with what does His rule contrast?

Nebuchadnezzar Vs. Belshazzar

Chapters 4 and 5 of Daniel are clearly linked in that they betray two approaches to the use of authority. There are good rulers and bad rulers. Rulers such as Nebuchadnezzar get things right when they humble themselves, acknowledge the overarching rule of God, and treat the things of God, the people of God, and their subjects with respect. Bad rulers, such as Belshazzar, refuse to humble themselves, don't acknowledge the overarching rule of God, and don't treat the things of God, the people of God, or their subjects with respect.

Nebuchadnezzar learned his lesson in chapter 4, but Belshazzar shook his fist willfully at God and refused to learn from his predecessor's experience (Dan. 5:18-21). He didn't give even a moment's thought to the God to whom he owed his existence, let alone his kingship. "Pride goes before destruction, and a haughty spirit before a fall" (Prov. 16:18; see Dan. 4:37).

 GOING FURTHER

Do the first five questions on your own.

1. Write down the relationships you are in, in which you have authority. Assess the manner in which you exercise your authority. Are you like God and Jesus, or are you like Nebuchadnezzar or Belshazzar?

2. In what areas do you fail to exercise authority in the way God expects?

3. What specific things will you do differently now?

4. Spend some time repenting of any misuse of your authority and asking God for help and wisdom in your future use of authority.

5. How can others in the group help you, either through prayer or with practical support?

6. If you are in a group, share what is appropriate from the first four questions. Spend some time talking and praying about the points raised in question 5.

6

The Beast and Beauty

DANIEL 7

Getting Some Perspective

The Historical Context

The first verse of Daniel 7 sets the historical context for us—Daniel's dream comes to him "in the first year of Belshazzar king of Babylon." This is significant for a number of reasons. It was probably the year in which Cyrus took over the Median empire on his way to the eventual overthrow of Babylon. While these were days of hope for many Israelites, it seems clear from chapters 10–12, which largely arise in the last days of the Babylonian empire and the first days of the Median/Persian empire, that Daniel didn't share their optimism.

Such thinking is not very surprising given what Daniel had witnessed of Belshazzar's reign. Perhaps his unprincipled, arrogant, and rebellious reign caused Daniel to think deeply on questions such as, "What will happen when people like Belshazzar are allowed to go on? What will things be like when their persecution of the people of God becomes unbearable? How can the people of God go on in a world where God no longer rescues them, where the flames consume them and lions tear them apart? If things do get worse, how will we grapple with them? How can we explain God? How can we live for Him in a world full of such fierce opposition to Him?"

The Literary Context

The literary style of Daniel 1–6 is familiar to us and easy enough to interpret. The same cannot be said for Daniel 7–12, so now is a good time to sketch in some background for our reading. The style of literature used in Daniel 7–12 has become known as "apocalyptic" literature, from the Greek word *apocalypse*, meaning "revelation." This literature began to appear around the time of the Exile. It was composed in and for times of trial, as a kind of private comfort for believers as they learned that things are not always all right on earth, and that the people of God are not always victorious or free from danger.

In addition to Daniel 7–12, as you read the Bible you will find pockets of apocalyptic literature tucked away in such places as Isaiah 24–27, Mark 13, and 2 Thessalonians 2. Zechariah in the Old Testament and Revelation in the New Testament are almost completely apocalyptic. Some of the telltale features of this sort of literature are:

- strange imagery (e.g., beasts, dragons, angels),

- constant flipping between what's happening in heaven and what's happening on earth,

- repetitive use of such numbers as three, three-and-a-half, four, six, seven, ten, twelve, and their equivalents (e.g., 1,260 days) or multiples,

- dreams and visions,

- reference to colors.

However, apocalyptic is not simply a literary style. It is also a philosophy of life and history—a worldview. Fundamental to apocalyptic thinking is that history moves in regular, recurring patterns or waves of events, spiraling toward the point where God will finally intervene in some dramatic way to wind up history, judge those in opposition to Him, and vindicate those faithful to Him. This is the world according to apocalyptic literature.

Many of us are familiar with some of the common ways of interpreting the apocalyptic literature of books such as Daniel and Revelation. People add up the years and try to make them fit various events in the past or present, and then predict what will happen in the (usually imminent!) future. They examine various people or nations and try to demonstrate that Daniel or John had those particular people or nations in mind when they wrote.

The danger in such an approach is that we can concentrate so much on one moment in history that we miss the main point of what apocalyptic literature is all about—the "big picture" of God's ways in the world. Apocalyptic literature says, "This is the way God always works in His world. Sure, it may get more intense toward the end of history, but what happens then will be just like what's happening now, so don't let it surprise you."

Getting to Daniel 7

 FINDING TRUTH

Read Daniel 7.

1. If you feel adventurous, try to draw the scene portrayed! (This may help you understand the passage.)

2. Describe in your own words how you would feel if you were Daniel when you dreamed about:

    ▲ the beasts

    ▲ God

3. The beasts obviously represent the rule of various kings or kingdoms in comparison with the rule of God. List the differences between the two:

The Beasts	God

4. How does Daniel react to his dream?

Statues and Images Yet Again

We started the book of Daniel by talking about a contest between the kingdom of God and human kingdoms. This has been a recurring theme throughout the book of Daniel, and it is related to our being made in the image of God. We could summarize the ideas like this:

▲ True human rule or authority is to be exercised as Adam was meant to exercise it—recognizing it as a gift from God, and imitating God's style of rule (just, merciful, and kind).

▲ Rule that does not recognize that it is delegated from God, and that does not imitate God's rule, is no longer true human rule. It is inhuman or beastly.

This background is fundamental for understanding Daniel 7. The important thing is not working out who the various kings or kingdoms are, but understanding what the style of their rule is. The first beast has occasional human characteristics (like Nebuchadnezzar). However, the last beast and the little horn that springs from it have little true humanity left in them. This "beastly" rule by four kingdoms is deliberately contrasted with the rule of the enigmatic "one like a son of man" (v. 13). This heavenly figure is also a human figure, who exercises his rule in a truly human way (i.e., under the overarching rule of God). This "son of man" is therefore a perfect man, one truly in the image of God—a new and perfect Adam.

Now that we've done this background work and have tried to understand what the term "son of man" might have meant in its original context, it's time to do what we've wanted to do ever since we first read the term "son of man," that is, think about Jesus.

 GOING FURTHER

1. Why might Jesus have used the term "son of man" to describe Himself?

Read Philippians 2:5-11.

2. How does Daniel, and particularly Daniel 7, help us understand this passage?

We haven't quite finished with the term "son of man" until we read the interpretation of Daniel's dream. In Daniel 7:1-14, the term "son of man" clearly refers to one individual who does what no human being has done before—lives and rules as the image of God. As a result, he receives what Adam received but forfeited—the right to rule forever over God's kingdom. In verses 15-28, however, the rule of God is given to "the saints, the people of the Most High." Daniel 4 and 5 told us that God is the one who "rules the kingdoms of men, giving them to whom he will." Although "whom he will" has first reference to the "son of man" or Jesus, it does not stop there. Here in

Daniel 7 and in other parts of the Bible, God speaks of other meek, humble, obedient human beings who have learned to accept God's overarching rule. And in Daniel 7, God promises that these people will inherit the earth (compare Matt. 5:5).

Seeing the Big Picture

 FINDING TRUTH

1. What was the situation of the Jewish people when Daniel saw the vision (refer to study 1 or read Psalm 137)?

2. What does Daniel 7 say about their future?

3. What purpose do you think the recording of Daniel's dream had for the people of Daniel's time and for those who followed?

4. What is the key verse of the passage? Why?

The picture of Daniel 7 is grand. As we said earlier, it gives a philosophy of life and history. It tells us that in history there are forces that are anti-God, that set themselves not only against God but also against His people. However, God is the King of the world. He is in control. He has always defeated and judged the forces of chaos and therefore His victory is assured in the future.

In addition, the saints of God should know that, although things may get worse, there will be an end. God will send His ideal ruler. This ruler's coming and presence will begin the judgment process that will finally result in God's victory, the vindication of God and His saints, and the saints receiving a kingdom from God.

Stephen sees this in Acts 7. With the enemies of Jesus arrayed against him, Stephen stands up for his Lord. And as Stephen is dying, God gives him an insight into heaven. Stephen looks up and sees Jesus standing as the heavenly Son of Man, at God's right hand, ruling and judging on God's behalf, seeing Stephen's suffering and assuring him of victory.

GOING FURTHER

1. Are there times in your life when you have felt completely overwhelmed by:

   ▲ the way the world is going;

   ▲ the way things are going for you because of the forces at work in the world; or

   ▲ the cost you have to pay for being a Christian?

   How does this passage encourage you as you face such circumstances?

2. How does the life, death, resurrection, and ascension of Jesus add to the message of Daniel 7 in this regard?

7

Rams, Goats, and Lambs

DANIEL 8

With Daniel 8 we move deep into apocalyptic literature. These chapters have produced all sorts of interesting speculation about the possible course of history. Numbers have been counted and identifications made. In this study we have a much more modest goal—to help you interpret this passage in such a way as to assist your approach to all such apocalyptic literature.

First we must notice how the chapter begins. Up until now we have spent most of our time in Babylon, the capital of the Babylonian empire under such kings as Nebuchadnezzar and Belshazzar. With Daniel 8 the setting changes. Daniel is moved in his vision to Susa, the winter residence of the Persian kings. In other words, this vision concerns the next great force in world history as far as it affects God's people—the Persian empire. Moreover, we are now in future time, far from the time of the Exile of the Jews in Babylon.

The second thing to notice is that, however strange the events are, the passage itself does provide some interpretation of those events—verses 1-14 tell the story, while verses 15-27 give some interpretation.

 FINDING TRUTH

Read Daniel 8.

In the following table we have listed crucial elements of the story told in verses 1-14. Write down the interpretation of those elements given in verses 15-27.

Vs.	Event/Person	Interpretation	Vs.
3	"I looked up, and there before me was a ram . . ."		
3	". . . with two horns."		
5	"Suddenly a goat with a prominent horn between his eyes came from the west."		
7	"I saw him attack the ram furiously, striking the ram and shattering his two horns."		
8	"The goat became very great, but at the height of his power his large horn was broken off, and in its place four prominent horns grew up."		
9	"Out of one of them came another horn, which started small but grew in power to the south and to the east and toward the Beautiful Land."		
10	"It grew until it reached the host of the heavens, and it threw some of the starry host down to the earth and trampled on them."		
11	"It set itself up to be as great as the Prince of the host; it took away the daily sacrifice from him, and the place of his sanctuary was brought low."		
12	"Because of the rebellion, the host of the saints and the daily sacrifice were given over to it. It prospered in everything it did, and truth was thrown to the ground."		

God's Patterns
Circles

One of the striking things about the Bible is that it is full of recurring patterns. These patterns become visible from the very first pages of the Bible. For example, the first chapter of Genesis tells us that God made the world and that He made it very good. The second and third chapters tell us that humans don't like the rule of God. They prefer self-rule, which God allows them to exercise to their own detriment. However, the closing verses of Genesis 3 tell us that God's judgment on our self-rule is one of mercy and grace (He clothes Adam and Eve and puts them out of the garden in order to stop their state of sin and judgment from becoming permanent). This cycle of grace, sin, judgment, and grace is repeated time and time again in the first eleven chapters of Genesis.

Patterns like this keep recurring in the Bible. Daniel is no exception. In the book of Daniel we have seen recurrent patterns of divine and human activity (remember the similarities we saw between Daniel 3 and 6).

The Bible appears to indicate that in God's world there are recurrent patterns of divine and human activity—given God's action, humans respond in characteristic ways, which in turn draws a characteristic divine response.

 FINDING TRUTH

1. Read the passages and fill in the table.

	Isaiah 14:12-23	Ezekiel 28:1-19
The focus of the passage	The king of Babylon	The king/ruler of Tyre
What is his chief sin?		
What if any impact will he have on the people of God?		
How does/will God respond?		

	Daniel 8:1-27	2 Thessalonians 2:1-12
The focus of the passage	"a stern-faced king"	"the man of lawlessness"
What is his chief sin?		
What, if any, impact will he have on the people of God?		
How does/will God respond?		

As you can see, the patterns we see in Daniel 8 are not new. They have been seen previously and they will be seen again.

From Beginning to End

The Bible not only tells us that God works in cyclical or recurrent patterns. The God of the Bible also works in a line— He starts at the beginning and works toward a particular end that He has in mind. He plans every event along the line with the end result in mind.

Apocalyptic: Combining God's Characteristic Patterns

Let's have a look at the two patterns of God's activity. The first pattern could be represented by a circle with a number of recurring points (e.g., God's grace, human sin, divine judgment, God's grace).

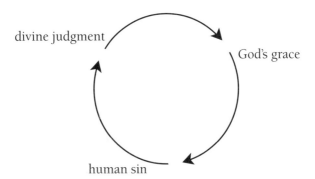

The second pattern could be represented by a line beginning at creation and progressing toward the end of history.

Apocalyptic writing appears to take these two ways that God works in the world and combine them, so that we get a sort of spiral toward that great climactic moment in history when everytning will come to its ultimate expression, as God intervenes to bring about the end of history.

Apocalyptic literature could be described as a section taken out of the spiral. It talks about a particular point in history and says that this is like a snapshot of where all history is going.

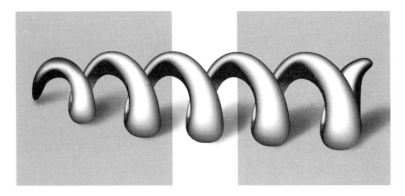

This is what is happening in Daniel 8. The events depicted here seem to refer to particular events in Jewish history. The ram represents the kings of Media and Persia (8:20). The goat is the king of Greece (8:21), from whom came four Greek kingdoms. The "stern-faced" king appears to refer specifically to the reign of a king called Antiochus Epiphanes in the second century B.C. In 167 B.C. this man, who believed himself to be the earthly manifestation of the Greek God *Zeus Olympios*, conquered Jerusalem and dedicated the temple in Jerusalem to his god. (In 9:27, this is called "the abomination that causes desolation.") The reference to 2,300 evenings and mornings (8:14) possibly refers to the time separating the appointment of a specific high priest and the rededication of the temple in 164 B.C.; it could also be an apocalyptic way of saying that there will be a fixed and limited period of time before God acts to vindicate His name and His servants, and that the sign of this will be the reconstruction of the temple.

If Daniel 7 is the broad canvas showing how God works in history and where He is headed, then Daniel 8 focuses in on one example of these forces at work and says that this is what the end of all history will look like.

GOING FURTHER

Apocalyptic literature teaches us about the final end of those who set themselves against God and His kingdom. It tells us these truths in vivid language and cataclysmic images; the Bible also sets out the same truths in plain language, but it is the same message in the end. With this in mind, read 2 Thessalonians 1:3-12.

1. What does God promise for those who don't know God and don't obey the Gospel?

2. What does God promise for those who have believed the apostle's testimony about Jesus (i.e., have believed the Gospel)?

3. What can we expect as we wait?

4. What sorts of things should we be praying for as we wait?

5. Spend some time praying about these things.

8

"O Lord, Hear and Act!"

DANIEL 9

 STARTING OUT

Read Jeremiah 25:8-11 and 29:10-14.

1. According to Jeremiah, why were the Israelites in Babylon?

   Did not listen to God's words

2. What had God promised to do after seventy years?

   Bring p— back / — land

3. What would be the stimulus for His actions?

   calling — ⚬ ·— / seeking. — / praying ! . —

How Long?

The big question of the last chapter we studied was "How long, O Lord?" Given the presence of persecution, the question is not surprising from a personal point of view. But the question is far more than a personal one. When godly people ask God, "How long?" they are not only doing so out of personal interest, but also out of concern for the glory of God. It is out of the same sort of concern that we pray, "Our Father in heaven, hallowed be your name," which is fundamentally a cry for God to end the dishonoring of His name. In Daniel, it is also a cry to God to fulfil His word and bring an end to all usurpers of His kingship, so that He alone might be King.

Perhaps it is with the question of "How long?" that Daniel found himself pondering the Scriptures in "the first year of the reign of Darius son of Xerxes" (9:1). Darius is probably one and the same as Cyrus. This is hinted at in the NIV footnote to 6:28, which notes that the translation can read, "Darius, that is, the reign of Cyrus." If this is right, then the first year of the reign of Darius/Cyrus would be an entirely appropriate time to be wrestling with prophecies about the return from exile, since prophets such as Isaiah had actually named Cyrus as the one who would be God's agent in bringing the people back to the Promised Land (see Isa. 44:28).

Note also that 9:1 takes us back to the time frame of 7:1 (see lesson 6, "The Historical Context").

 FINDING TRUTH

Read Daniel 9.

1. How does Daniel practice and describe praying?

    confessing 9; sins / sins of Israel
    Requesting. God's mercy /; names sake
    Acknowledging God's righteousness

2. What emotions are evident in his words?

    shame, humility

3. List the descriptions of God.

Merciful, righteous, awesom, forgiving mighty

4. List the descriptions of the people.

Sinful, wicked, rebellious, covered w/ shame unfaithful, object y scorn

5. If you are in a group, allocate the following verses around the group and have each person or group summarize the passage. Look for the essence of what is being said.

Verses:

4-6

7-11

12-14

15-16

17-19

Daniel's Attitude in Praying

A number of things about Daniel's attitude as he prays are helpful models for us in our prayers:

▲ He prays with seriousness, throwing his whole person into it ("I turned to the Lord God and pleaded with him in prayer and petition, in fasting, and in sackcloth and ashes"—v. 3.).

▲ He acknowledges his solidarity with the people he is praying for ("*we* have sinned . . ."—vv. 5ff.).

▲ He prays as a representative of and on behalf of his people (v. 17).

▲ He prays on the basis of God's promises (God had promised to hear and forgive when His people humbled themselves and prayed on the basis of the temple in Jerusalem—2 Chron. 6:36-39).

▲ He affirms and acknowledges that God is righteous in all His actions (v. 7).

 GOING FURTHER

1. What can we learn from this prayer about the nature of Daniel's relationship with God? *knows what God has promised, know what God wants, is highly esteemed because of answered prayer*

2. What does Daniel's prayer (vv. 4-19) and God's response (vv. 20-27) tell us about God? *God does what he says*

3. Why do you think this prayer is recorded in the Bible?

God's Answer to Daniel's Prayer

While Daniel is still praying to God, God sends the answer to his prayer through Gabriel. Gabriel comes to Daniel "in swift flight" (v. 21). Daniel's prayer had been the prayer of the godly, and Gabriel assures him that "as soon as you began to pray, an answer was given."

For us, however, the answer is hardly enlightening at first sight. If we consider the context it becomes easier. The first half of Daniel's prayer had focussed on sin and the need for forgiveness. Verse 24 answers this part of Daniel's prayer and promises that sin and punishment will be done away with.

The second half of Daniel's prayer focused on the restoration of God's honor through the restoration of His people and His city. Whatever the numbers mean in verses 25-27, the main point of them is to assure Daniel that God is in control and that there will be an end to all the desolation and sacrilege. At the appropriate moment God will vindicate His name and the people who are called by His name.

God is asking Daniel to understand that He is behind the processes of history, and that He will not delay in answering the prayers of all who long for forgiveness, justice, and an end to the dishonoring of God and the persecution of His people.

Every time we pray the Lord's prayer, we line ourselves up with Daniel as we ask God to "hallow" His name and to bring in His kingdom. And through Daniel God promises us that He will do just that—at the appropriate time.

 **GOING FURTHER**

Gabriel's answer must have been difficult for Daniel. All his life he and his fellow Jews had waited for God to deal with Nebuchadnezzar. They had longed for the day of forgiveness and atonement for the sins that had brought them into exile. The answer Gabriel brings is that, although there will be a return from exile, the day of realization of all of God's purposes is still a long way off. Eventually Daniel died without seeing the answer to his prayers.

1. How would you feel in Daniel's situation?

2. Are you willing to not always see the answer to your prayers in this lifetime, yet still believe in the God of history?

3. What do you pray for (or should you pray for) that might not be answered in your lifetime?

4. Read Hebrews 11. What does it say to people like Daniel and us about this problem?

9

The Awesome Vision
DANIEL 10–12

Chapters 10–12 of Daniel belong together and concern one particular revelation given to Daniel. It is the longest single section of the book. Many of the details we will learn in these chapters will be things we have already read about in chapter 8. And yet, much of what we read in chapters 10–12 will seem very obscure—we won't be sure who is being spoken about or where some of the places are or what exactly is going on.

In 10:14 we read that the events depicted in this chapter concern "a time yet to come" for the Jewish people. As it happens, these events bear a striking resemblance to events that occurred in the second century B.C., as recorded in Jewish and other reliable historical sources. In the pages that follow we have outlined this story along with the verse references from Daniel, so that you can read the history and also follow it through in Daniel.

 FINDING TRUTH

Daniel 10–12 are difficult chapters to get your mind around, and to help deal with this we'll investigate it in a slightly different way.

Work through the following summary of the chapters: First, read each set of verses; then, read our summary of the historical events to which the verses apparently refer (or, in some cases, our best guess as to the correct interpretation of the verses).

Daniel 10:3, 14

It is the third year of Cyrus, king of Persia, and Daniel is deep in prayer. In response to his prayers, God sends a messenger to instruct him and to outline future history for him.

Daniel 11:2-4

The Persian kings of Daniel's time will be overthrown by a mighty Greek king, Alexander the Great (11:3).

Alexander will die early, leaving an empire to be divided among four generals. Two of the kingdoms that spring out of this division will become prominent—Egypt in the South and Syria in the North.

Daniel 11:5-28

These two kingdoms will war against each other, attempt alliances, and act treacherously with each other. There will even be a time of peace between them. However, eventually a particular king in the North will be murdered, and his natural successor will be prevented from coming to the throne by the quick action of a usurper, Antiochus Epiphanes IV. This contemptible person will depose and murder the current Jewish high priest, seizing rich lands and acquiring wealth. He will make two campaigns against Egypt and will plot to destroy his nephew in the South.

Antiochus will also resolve to destroy all those in Palestine who are loyal to God's covenant with His people. To this end, Antiochus will stop at the Holy City, Jerusalem, on his way back from Egypt, and will enter the temple and plunder its sacred treasures.

His second campaign against Egypt in the South will bring Antiochus face to face with the Romans, who will stop him from waging war against Egypt. Fresh from this rebuff, he will decide to strengthen his rule at home by making his citizens fully Greek. This program will start with dissident Jews who have given up God's covenant with Moses.

Daniel 11:29-32

Antiochus will then act to stop the daily sacrifice in the temple, knowing that only faithful Jews will resist. They will resist as expected, even under brutal persecution, pillaging, death, and imprisonment. Nevertheless, the persecution against them will continue.

Daniel 11:36-39

The faithful Jews will not be rescued by divine intervention as Daniel and his friends had been, although they will receive a little help (perhaps through the encouragement of the first Judean guerrillas and activists).

At this point the picture painted by the angel becomes quite fuzzy and unclear to us. Like all those who step out from under the King of heaven's rule, this king will claim to be God, doing as he pleases. He will succeed, but only until God chooses to put an end to it.

Daniel 11:40-45

Yet again the details become hard for us to understand. The messenger's telescopic lens focuses even more on the distant future, stating that there will be opposition and the falling of many nations. There will be an affront against the people of God and the land of God's people, a subsequent retreat, and the death of this one who sets himself against the King of heaven and against the people of the King of heaven.

Daniel 12:1-3

In this last great battle there will be many deaths. The godly and ungodly alike will die. Together they will sleep in the dust of the earth, and together they will awake from sleep to judgment.

The wise, who have feared God and turned many to a right relationship with the God of heaven, will awake to everlasting life. They will shine like the stars forever and ever.

On the other hand, the godless, who have rejected the King of heaven, will wake to everlasting contempt and disgrace.

1. Imagine that you were a Jew in this time of persecution and trial. What questions would you want to ask God?

2. Reread Daniel 12:4-13.

   a. What questions does Daniel ask God's messenger?

   b. What answer/s does Daniel receive?

(Note that, although the numbers at the end of Daniel 12 can be figured in such a way as to fit various events at the time of Antiochus, this doesn't appear to be the main point. The main point appears to be that persecution will occur and will at times seem unlimited. Nevertheless, it is limited by God, and the wise person, knowing this, should endure for that extra period. When the time has come, God will act to end persecution and to deliver and vindicate His saints.)

The Problem of Suffering

 GOING FURTHER

Think about this passage and the whole book of Daniel; answer these questions on the basis of what the book says about God.

1. Does God care for His people and always have their best interests in mind?

2. Is God so great that He can do whatever He pleases, whenever He pleases, with whomever He pleases?

3. Does God allow His people to suffer, even to the point of death?

The problem of suffering is presented starkly in the book of Daniel. To most of us it might seem somewhat inconsistent to answer yes to all of the above questions. We think that if God were really good and great, He would not allow His people to suffer. When we see His people suffering, we come to one of several conclusions:

- ▲ God is not really good. He doesn't always have our best interests in mind.

- ▲ God is not really great. He is not really in control of the world but is somewhat restricted by the actions of people in the world.

- ▲ The suffering is happening because we humans have not done some action that would have averted suffering.

But the Bible doesn't allow us to use any of these excuses. This is clear in Daniel. God is good; God is great; and yet God *does* allow His people to suffer.

So, how do we think about this? What do we do? How do we answer our critics, let alone our own doubts and questions?

As Christians we must start at the right point. Rather than looking at the despair that we or our friends are suffering, we must turn to the center of our faith—to the unjust suffering and pain of our Lord Jesus Christ. If we do this we will find a solid rock on which to stand.

The first thing we find in the Cross of Jesus is that God isn't detached from suffering. He is not remote and aloof as He sometimes appears to be (notice that, although He is said to be present with Daniel and his friends in their hour of need, we don't see many references to His immediate presence in chapter 11). In the suffering of Jesus on the Cross, God absorbs suffering into His own life. He experiences it from the inside. The end result is that He knows our suffering as a fellow sufferer.

The second thing we find in the Cross is that God isn't defeated or overcome by suffering. Jesus comes back from the dead. He is raised. God is indeed great and good. Wickedness brings suffering and death, but God can bring life against these things and win. We see this also in Daniel 12:1-3. Evil appears to triumph in chapter 11, but in chapter 12 God rescues His people and vindicates them.

But the Resurrection is not just vindication of God and His people. The Resurrection of Jesus is also the first installment of the new world—a world in which righteousness dwells and where suffering, pain, grief, and death no longer exist. The point is that suffering cannot defeat God's good purposes for me. His great goodwill toward me is seen in the Cross and will be vindicated at last.

 GOING FURTHER

1. Does Daniel 10–12 describe any *positive* features of suffering as far as God's people are concerned?

Read Romans 5:1-5.

2. What do these verses imply will be the normal lot of those seeking to live the Christian life?

3. Read 2 Corinthians 4:7-12, 16-18. What does this passage tell us about Paul's attitude toward the inevitable suffering that came upon him as an apostle? What, for Paul, were the positive features or outcomes of this suffering?

4. When things are going badly for you because of your resolve to be a Christian, what is your first reaction? What have you learned in this study that might change that reaction?

FAITHWALK
BIBLE STUDIES

Ask your local bookstore about these other
FaithWalk Bible Studies

Beginnings
Eden and Beyond: Genesis 1–11

Deuteronomy
The Lord Your God

Isaiah
The Road to God

The Beatitudes
A Guide to Good Living: Matthew 5:1-12

Galatians
The Gospel of Grace

Ephesians
Our Blessings in Christ

1 Timothy
The Household of God

Notes

Notes

Notes

Notes

About Matthias Media

This Bible study guide, part of the *FaithWalk Bible Studies,* was originally developed and published in Australia by Matthias Media. Matthias Media is an evangelical publisher focusing on producing resources for Christian ministry. For further information about Matthias Media products, visit their website at: www.matthiasmedia.com.au; or contact them by E-mail at: matmedia@ozemail.com.au; or by fax at: 61-2-9662-4289.